What's In My Pocket?

Pocket, pocket,
what's in my pocket?

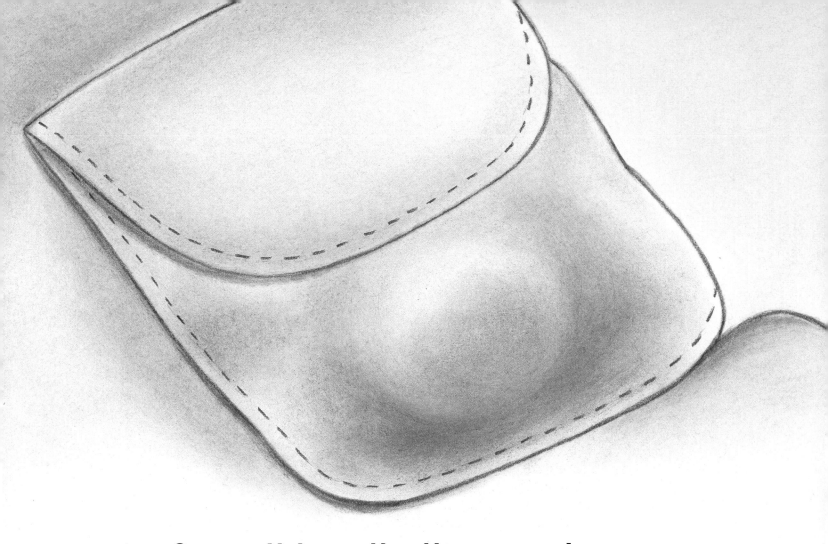

Something that's round.

3

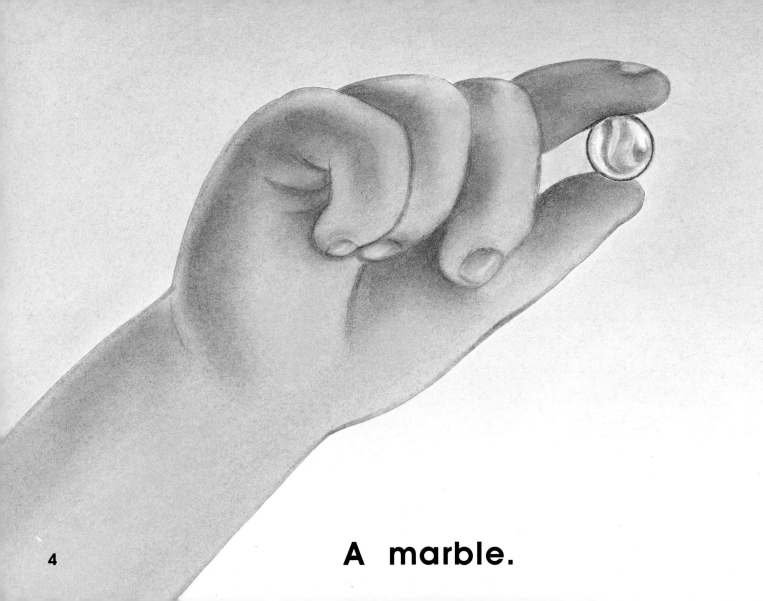

4

A marble.

Pocket, pocket,
what's in my pocket?
Something that's square.

5

A block.

Pocket, pocket,
what's in my pocket?
Something that's soft.

A feather.

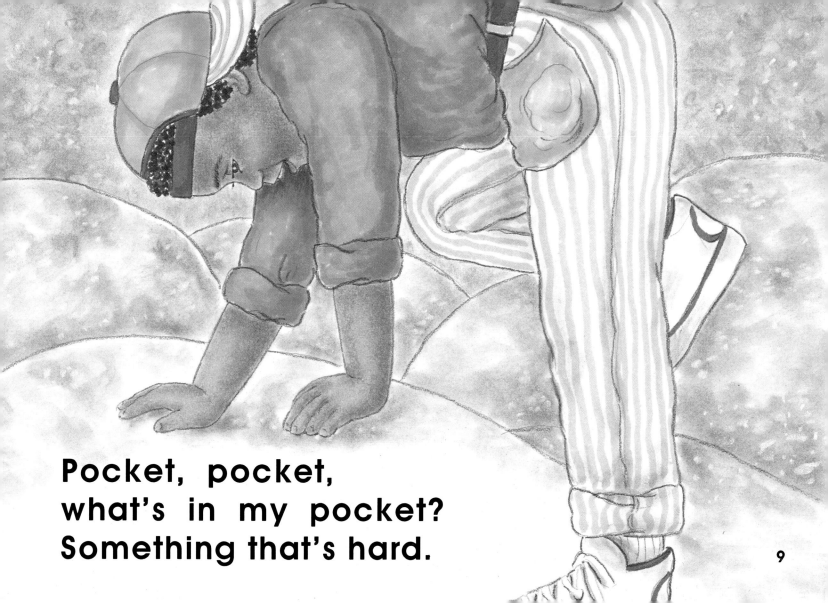

Pocket, pocket,
what's in my pocket?
Something that's hard.

9

A rock.

Pocket, pocket,
what's in my pocket?
Something that's fuzzy.

11

A bear.

Pocket, pocket,
what's in my pocket?
Something that's gooey.

13

A worm.

Pocket, pocket,
what's in *my* pocket?